Rambling Thoughts from my
Twenty-Something Self

To Pat:
Enjoy!

Rambling Thoughts from my Twenty-Something Self

Josh K. Stevens

Copyright © 2025 by Josh K. Stevens
All rights reserved. No part of this book may be reproduced in any manner whatsoever without written permission except in the case of brief quotations embodied in critical articles and reviews.
First Printing, 2025

Cover Artwork done by August K. Stevens

Thanks to those of you who hung with me during the
time these poems were written...
I was insufferable.

To anyone who's going through tough times,
You got this... It'll all be okay.

And to Penny and Gus, don't bottle it up...
if you ever need to vent, I'm always here for you.

CONTENTS

	DEDICATION	iv
1	Demise	1
2	Great Gray Beast	2
3	Fantasy	4
4	Biggest Porch	7
5	Unattainable	10
6	California	11
7	Fairy Tale	15
8	Thoughts From a Diner While Waiting	23
9	When Will It Be	25
10	Subconscious	26
11	Take a Gamble	29
12	Chasm	32
13	Realizations	38
14	Monster Face	43
15	On My Lips	45
16	Real Rain Came	47

| 17 | Rambling | 49
| 18 | Lost | 51
| 19 | Life, From a Different Point of View | 53
| 20 | Idiotic | 55
| 21 | Finis | 57
| 22 | Goodbye, Cruel World | 59
| 23 | Fascination | 61
| 24 | Black Hole | 63
| 25 | Dread | 65
| 26 | "Apocalypse" | 68
| 27 | A Chance Meeting in the Woods | 70
| 28 | Another Day | 72
| 29 | Pinocchio | 74

1

Demise

Wait for a second
    For the sound of the city
To come crashing down around you
Like a firebomb
At Dresden
Just wait
Wait for it
Just wait

2

Great Gray Beast

Wind is rushing
    At my back
Trying to shove me
Trying to make me fall
Raindrops are falling
Blinding me
Soaking me through
Straight to the bone
The city lights are blinding
Cars pass
Lights disappear
Sweat is pouring
Off my body
I've been running for months
Now I am standing
On a thin brick ledge
Slick with rain
And crumbling
Trying my hardest
To thwart what lies behind me
Snarling and gnashing

In the filthy room
On the other side
Of the window at my back.
I thought I was in the clear
I thought I had escaped
But the Great Grey Beast
Has come to find me
I am mere inches
From turning around
Climbing back inside
And allowing it to devour me
Ravish me
Tear me apart
Bleed me dry
But I don't know
If I can allow myself
To feel its razor-sharp teeth
Sink into the nape of my neck
Once again.

3

Fantasy

Every night I dream
    You are in my vision
  Your voice plays endlessly
   I fall in love with you all over again

Every night I dream
We dance in a field of roses
'Neath the pale moon beams
I hold you tightly in my arms
As close as I possibly can
Feeling our hearts beating in unison
And whisper in your ear
For hours upon hours
Until the sun begins to break the dawn
We gaze into each
    other's eyes
I fall in love with you all over again

Every night I dream
We sit on a blanket
At a solid white sand beach

At the edge of the breaking surf
Alone except for one another
Watch the fog roll in
The
   tides move in and out
Your head on my shoulder
I kiss your cheek
And fall in love with you all over again

Every night I dream
We are sitting on a hilltop
Watching an endless display of fireworks
I take your hand in mine
Feeling the silken skin
I look at you
The happiness in your face is radiant
More so than the fireworks
Against the velvet sky
And I fall in love with you all over again

Every night I dream
We are in floating through Venice
In a gondola
Cuddling together as the stars hover above
Fireflies waltz around us
I whisper sweet nothings in your ear
As an Italian love song wraps around us
And I fall in love with you all over again

Every night I dream
Always about you

| 6 | - FANTASY

Always about the wonderful girl you are
The way you make me feel
The way you make me happy
How little I deserve you
How I ever lived before I met you
And I fall in love with you all over again

Every night I dream
And every morning I awake and find you
I can't help but smile because you are here with me
I want to be with you forever
I want to be the one you love
You stretch and yawn and look at me
And reach out and touch me
And you speak and sooth me with your words
And I gaze upon you
And I fall in love with you all over again.

4

Biggest Porch

The party around me
    Keeps dragging on
People Arrive
And they park on the lawn
The bands final number
Still ringing like a gong
I hold in my hand
This bottle of rum
It was good, then warm
Now almost gone
Not in the mood
To be around everyone
Gotta work in the morning
Come the rise of the sun
The a.m.'s approaching
I know I should run
So I say my goodbyes
To every last one
But you take my hand
And tell me to come
I start to smoke

BIGGEST PORCH

You say you want one
You pull me outside
The night's far from done.
'Cuz underneath this cloudy sky
This night without a moon
On the biggest porch I've ever seen
Having a heart to heart with you
Nothing beneath me matters at all
Smoking cigarettes two by two
On the biggest porch I've ever seen
Having a heart to heart with you.
When I awake tomorrow
In my sunlit colorless room
Everything will be the same
Including me and you.
The world, the problems
The sky, the clouds,
The stars, the sun, the moon.
Can't be changed by dreamers
In an hour or two.
But tonight it feels better
Leaning next to you.
If we had an eternity
I would like to assume
You'd chase away the darkness
Of my self inflicted doom.
Now the night is fading
Dawn is coming soon.
A single night is not enough
To rectify a ruin.
'Cuz underneath this cloudy sky

This night without a moon
On the biggest porch I've ever seen
Having a heart to heart with you
Nothing beneath me matters at all
Smoking cigarettes two by two
On the biggest porch I've ever seen
Having a heart to heart with you.

5

Unattainable

Every single day
    In so many uncountable ways
My entire life is changing
The storm clouds are breaking
The rain is ceasing
I begin to see daylight again
I know what a bird feels
As it pecks through it's shell
To embrace the world around it
As it crashes in
And it's all because of you.

6

California

She left
    After changing me completely
To wander the land
Like a nomad
In pursuit
Of the beast
She longed to tame
A dream
She longed to live
And somewhere
In an oasis
Just beyond
The deserts sandy reaches
She found it
Settled with it
And left me behind
With nothing more than
Emptiness and
My longing
Searching the horizon
Endlessly

– CALIFORNIA

For a sign
Knowing that
The sun never sets
On California
No matter how hard
It rains
In Chicago.
I watched
The landscape changed
People come and gone
Different jobs
Different locale
I sat
Waiting for her return.
Six years
Before she came back
Blowing in
Like a gust from the ocean
Amidst the tediousness
Of this everyman's everyday
Chiseling the frown
From my stone face
And replacing it
With a makeshift smile
I follow her
Or she follows me
I can't tell which
My head is spinning
Here in the dark
I feel everything
I felt originally

But somehow
I feel more
Kneeling
On the cobblestone
Kissing the face of an angel
Gazing up at her
Holding her
On the pedestal
She doesn't want to be on.
It seems surreal
This chance
Allowing me to reveal
My heart
My soul
And the fact that
My very existence is
Solely because of her
Good or Bad.
The bell tolls
I have only a flash
Give or take
Before the winds change
And she sets her sails
For her paradise
1800 miles away
I have to change time
I have to convince her
My throat is corroded
From all things
Left unsaid
I can't speak now

I can't do anything
I would fight for her
Beyond that
I would die for her
But in this instant
I have forgotten
How to breathe
How to think
How to move
The breeze picks up
Gust
I blink
She's gone again
All that is left is her pedestal
I dust it off
Place it back
On the shelf
In my heart
And wait for the sun
To rise anew.

7

Fairy Tale

I have been walking
    For weeks
Through her sunny field
Filled with brightly blossoming flowers,
Their sweet perfume
Makes it easier to breathe.
The sunlight,
Which had been missing
From my life,
Feels perfect
Upon my face.
I realize I am carrying something else
That feels pleasantly out of place,
Something that I haven't had
In my possession for some time.
Spreading across my lips,
I feel a smile
As it emerges from hiding
It radiates over my entire body
And I feel good
Better than I have for quite sometime

FAIRY TALE

I feel perfect
And I know that her field
And the sunlight
And the flowers
Are the reason for my happiness.
Now, I am standing at a chasm
Overlooking a deep valley,
Dark and black,
And I am Frighteningly overwhelmed
By its seemingly infinite vastness.
Below me, near an empty river bed,
Surrounded by skeletal remains
Of those who once were,
I see all of my fears
I see all of her fears
They push and pull
Against one another
Trying hard to stop me in my path,
All while a maniacal laughing being
Watches from the shadows.
For one moment
I am afraid,
Wanting badly to run away,
Knowing that she
Wants to do the same.
I look over my shoulder
Behind me, where I came from.
I see the vast beauty of her field,
With its lush green grass
Its blooming flowers
Its warm sunlight

It is the picture of purest perfection.
Beyond the field
Lay a forest
Which I had trekked through
Before arriving here,
The edge of the forest
That lay closest to her field,
Was layered in shades
Of black and gray,
Menacing and foreboding.
I remembered the dead trees
Standing motionless
In the forest
I remembered that there had been no sunlight
For months
I remembered that there had been no happiness
In that portion of the forest.
I remembered the pains I had encountered
The thorns, the insects, the animals
I remembered that I had to press on
To continue moving deeper,
The thorns gashing at my face
My hands, my arms
Their sharp points cutting me
To my soul
And drawing blood
For what seemed like ages,
Afraid that the forest
Would never end
And yet
Though it was filled

FAIRY TALE

With emptiness and broken dreams
It was familiar
So it was safe
And I was equally afraid
That the forest would end.
While I moved through
The broken sticks and gray trunks,
The thorn twists that were stealing my existence,
I was afraid of the forest,
I was afraid of what lay beyond.
I paused, looking at the forest
Looming on the horizon
Beyond me.
I had been afraid
To leave the comfortable pain
Because I didn't know
What lay ahead,
I realized that her field
Had been what loomed ahead.
Pure and utter joy
Had been what loomed ahead.
She
Had been what loomed ahead
She
Had made me feel
Like a better person than I was.
She
Had helped to heal the wounds
And nurture me back to health.
She
Had spoken to me

And hypnotized me with her words
She
Was perfect
She
Had been what lay beyond the forest
And she had been beautiful
Sweet
Caring
Kind
Smart
Fun
Interesting
And I was happy
To take her hand
And allow her to pull me
From the shadows of the forest
And into her field.
I turned back
To the chasm
And looked beyond
The great, wide, shadowy beast
Trying to glimpse at what lay beyond it.
I could see two roads,
Far in the distance.
One road weaved its way
Into a dark and desolate forest
And disappeared instantly
So that I could not see what lay
Beyond the trees.
The other road
Made its way to the base of a mountain.

FAIRY TALE

It spiraled around the base
Climbing higher and higher with every inch,
Climbing out of the chasm
Out of the shadows
Moving back into the sunlight.
At the top of the mountain
Lay a meadow
Filled with lush greens
And bright flowers
In the middle of the meadow
Set high above the mountain top
Stood a shining castle
Perfectly unblemished
Not a scratch
Not a dent
Not a speck of dirt
It was a beacon of hope
Filled with happiness
Filled with perfection
And she could be there
And I could be there
And we could be together
To hold each other
To kiss each other
To be with each other
To love each other
Unconditionally.
I paused
Briefly
Looking behind me at the forest
Looking behind me at her field

Looking ahead at the chasm
Looking down at the valley
Looking ahead at the options
Looking ahead at the forest
Looking ahead at the mountain
And the meadow
And the castle
And the option for pure happiness.
Looking ahead for her.
I was afraid
Of what may happen
On the journey through the chasm
Things could grow terrible
Things could make me unhappy
There may be thorns
There may be darkness
There could be all sorts
Of frightening creatures lurking in the shadows
Waiting to lash out and hurt me
Torture me
Kill me.
But things could also be good.
I thought about the prospects
The very shred of possibility
Of happiness
Of perfection
Of beauty
But most of all
Of her.
Of being with Her
Of sharing memories with Her

- FAIRY TALE

Of laying next to her
Of gazing upon her
Of watching her sleep
Of touching her face
Of kissing her lips
Her cheek
Her hands
Her nose
Her neck
Her body
Of feeling her love for me
Of loving her
Unconditionally.
I drew in a deep breath
I steadied my shaking hands
I swallowed the lump in my throat
I wiped the perspiration from my brow
And I began to climb down the rocky chasm
To the valley of shadow
To begin my quest
Hoping that it ended
Atop the mountain
In the meadow
In the kingdom
Of unconditional love
With her.

8

Thoughts From a Diner While Waiting

What do you feel when you commence into darkness?
    What do you see as your last breath draws nigh?
How do you act when you see that white light?
Who do you call when you know you will die?
When the bright shining light
Is all you can see
And the ones you love gather
Each sad eye weeping,
When the last thought you have
Is closing your eyes
Knowing this time
You won't wake from sleeping,
What is there to do when all's said and done?
Do you shrink to the shadows?
Do you turn tail and run?
Do you rage against it? Do you go unquiet?
Do you fight what is coming? Do you explode into riot?
Do you go silent and slowly and take what you have?
Enter heaven or hell, were you good or bad?
What type of box will you stay in forever?

Where do you want to be kept in the ground?
A blanket of dirt, a pillow of stone,
That's all you're allowed when you travel alone.
People may gather
People may not
People throw flowers
People may dab
Tears from their eyes, so sadness will go
People in black, their fine mourning clothes.
Will people miss you?
Will you be forgotten?
While lying in the ground
Cold and rotten?
The question remains
On all of our tongues,
The question still stands
On everyone's lips.
What does it mean,
This eternal slumber?
What does it feel
To be six feet under?

9

When Will It Be

One day we all awake
    And find ourselves not there
One day we'll all be lonely
My day's already here
One day we'll all be happy
My day has come and gone
One day we sit and we await
The day when we'll be done
One day we feel hatred
It's already in my heart
One day we all feel pain
It tears my soul apart
One day we all feel hurt
Each move makes my head sting
One day we'll all close our eyes
And never open them again
One day we all sit patiently
And await to take that ride
One day we all awake
And find ourselves not there.

10

Subconscious

Dreams just fade away
    But oddly life remains
Hope to find a meaning
Nothing ever seems to fit
Meet new people day by day
You will grow close
Then fall apart
They will go east
You will go west
Funny how it all works out
You will try
Your whole life through
To become somebody
Who's special
You will try
To make the world love you
To make the world view you
As a friend
Time counts down
It always does
Soon enough

You will be at the end
All those people who you knew
Will not recall who you are
As you lie dying
By Yourself
Reflecting
On the way things could have been
Should have been
They told you
You knew you would fail
They told you
You were not that great
They told you
Your dreams were too big
They told you
Never a word of encouragement
They killed the dreams you birthed
Like rabid beasts
From the womb of your mind
They left you in a dark corner
The darkness is moving in
To be closer to you
This is the place you have always feared
You can't help but look
Over your shoulder
At the past
The life behind you
You have failed at life
You have no friends
You have no family
You have no wife

- SUBCONSCIOUS -

You have no kids
You have no one who cares for you
You have no one to lean on
You have wishes for different choices
Wishes that things had gone differently
Wishes there were an easier way out
Maybe you did this to yourself
Maybe you should have
You didn't have the guts
That was up to you
Or maybe it was up to everyone else.
Darkness
Silence
Nothing
Dreams just fade away
But oddly life remains

11

Take a Gamble

No pain
    No stake
No wager
I should've tried
Instead I stand
Against the wall
In the murky caverns
Of my own existence.
Tell her how you feel
You want to love her
I should've tried
I would've failed
The words
Rest calmly
Upon my tongue
In my mouth
They shy away
When I open it
To speak
Scared
Of her reaction

TAKE A GAMBLE

What she'll say
I should've tried
I have no courage
No self respect
I don't expect respect
From others
Afraid of answers
I offer no questions
Afraid of questions
I seek no answers
Silence is bliss
The road to failure
Begins with attempt
The road to death
Begins with birth
My exit is up
Around the corner
What do I have to show
I should've tried
Intimidation
This girl makes me wonder
Over think
I should be content
With what I have
Friendship
I should've tried
Now the same old story
Played out again
With a brand new cast of characters
Me silent
She walks away

Out the door
Across the street
Out of my life
Into her car
Straight on down the highway.
Leaving me
Alone
In a private hell
I've created
No exits
I should've tried.

12

Chasm

I stand overlooking a chasm
A hole in the ground, nothing more
I can see straight across the chasm
There she stands, the girl I adore
The chasm is deep and inky
So dark that I can't see the floor
I stand here can't help but thinking
That I've been at this chasm before.

I want to close my eyes and jump
To leap over the infinite dark
To hide all my scars, my fears, my woes
I want to fill up her heart.
I know she wants to do the same
To leap over the infinite dark
To hide her scars, her fears, her woes
And Allow me to fill up her heart.

And I can, Yes I can
'Cause I know she's the one
I know that I must and I will

And I can, yes I can
I won't rest 'til I'm done.
I won't finish 'til her heart is filled

I can see her across the chasm
She's waving to me as I stand
She can hear me across the chasm
Telling her to take my hand
I don't want to be the first one to move
But then again neither does she
I don't want to leap and fall to the bottom
It needs to be done equally.

I want to close my eyes and jump
To leap over the infinite dark
To hide all my scars, my fears, my woes
I want to fill up her heart.
I know she wants to do the same
To leap over the infinite dark
To hide her scars, her fears, her woes
And Allow me to fill up her heart.

And I can, Yes I can
'Cause I know she's the one
I know that I must and I will
And I can, yes I can
I won't rest 'til I'm done.
I won't finish 'til her heart is filled

The longer I stand at the chasm
And watch her stare into my eyes

- CHASM

The less afraid I become of the chasm
Sprout wings from my back and I'll fly
I can tell she's a little bit taken
By the feelings I hold in my chest
I would pull them all out to wear on my sleeve
For one single tender caress.

I want to close my eyes and jump
To leap over the infinite dark
To hide all my scars, my fears, my woes
I want to fill up her heart.
I know she wants to do the same
To leap over the infinite dark
To hide her scars, her fears, her woes
And Allow me to fill up her heart.

And I can, Yes I can
'Cause I know she's the one
I know that I must and I will
And I can, yes I can
I won't rest 'til I'm done.
I won't finish 'til her heart is filled

As I study her from 'cross the chasm
I can tell she is feeling like me
She is longing to move past the chasm
To swim in my arms like the sea
She's afraid 'cause she can't see clearly
'Cause we're so very far apart
And I know if she'd just look closer
She'd see I could fill up her heart

CHASM

I want to close my eyes and jump
To leap over the infinite dark
To hide all my scars, my fears, my woes
I want to fill up her heart.
I know she wants to do the same
To leap over the infinite dark
To hide her scars, her fears, her woes
And Allow me to fill up her heart.

And I can, Yes I can
'Cause I know she's the one
I know that I must and I will
And I can, yes I can
I won't rest 'til I'm done.
I won't finish 'til her heart is filled

As I stand overlooking the chasm
It is suddenly simple to see
I nod as I size up the chasm
And I know that it's all up to me.
I grit my teeth and step forward
Close my eyes and can no longer see
I jump straight out into the darkness
Will wings sprout so they can carry me?

I want to close my eyes and jump
To leap over the infinite dark
To hide all my scars, my fears, my woes
I want to fill up her heart.
I know she wants to do the same

| 36 | – CHASM

To leap over the infinite dark
To hide her scars, her fears, her woes
And Allow me to fill up her heart.

And I can, Yes I can
'Cause I know she's the one
I know that I must and I will
And I can, yes I can
I won't rest 'til I'm done.
I won't finish 'til her heart is filled

I stood overlooking the chasm
A hole in the ground, nothing more
I could see straight across the chasm
Where she stood, the girl I adore
The chasm was deep and inky
So dark that could not see the floor
I feel the wind rushing straight at my face
A feeling I've never felt before

I closed my eyes and jumped
To leap over the infinite dark
I hid my scars, my fears, my woes
To attempt to fill up her heart.
I know she wanted to do the same
To leap over the infinite dark
To hide her scars, her fears, her woes
To Allow me to fill up her heart.

And I will, Yes I will
'Cause I know she's the one

I know that I can and I will
And I can, yes I can
I won't rest 'til I'm done.
I won't finish 'til her heart is filled

13

Realizations

You
    Left the girl you loved
Because she
was out and about
Hitting up Bars
With a Cro-Magnon Girl
With a big fat ass
And a big fat chin
And big fat hairy knuckles
And a big fat mouth
And she should have
A big fat brand across
Her big fat forehead
That says
"I am a big fat fucking hick."
You are not attractive.
You are not funny.
You are not as good as you think you are.
You are not Loretta Lynn.
You are not Patsy Cline.
You are not June Carter Cash.

You are not even Shania Twain.
You are a big fat slob.
You do Karaoke at "Cheeseburger in Paradise."
You are Thirty Fucking Years Old.
You live with your parents.
You think, because you got a gig at a speedway, you are great.
You are sorely mistaken.
Fuck you.
May your diaphragm rupture while you sing
And Madonna may defecate on your lifeless body.
You
Left the girl you loved
Because she
was out and about
Galivanting
With Honky Tonk Mother Fuckers
Whose only concern was being dumb
While Fucking and fighting
With their peanut sized brains
And their large upper bodies
And their wife beater t-shirts
With their stupid fucking slogans
"Save a horse, ride a cowboy."
You are not from Texas.
You do not rope cattle.
You have never ridden a horse.
You are not Johnny Cash.
You are not Marty Robbins
You are not Hank Williams.
You are not Charlie Daniels.
You are a Midwesterner.

You listen to shitty pop-country bullshit.
You think you are impressive.
You are not.
Fuck them all.
May your maggot infested corpses
Burn in eternal Hellfire while Billy Ray Cyrus plays on the radio.
You
You Left the girl you loved
Because she
Was Working out
With a Half-wit wrestler
Who parades himself around
Wearing tights, bragging about concussions
Being a jerk-off.
You are not Macho.
You are not a tough guy.
You are not in the WWF.
You are not "The Ultimate Warrior."
You are not "Hulk Hogan"
You are not "Macho Man Randy Savage."
You are not "The Rock."
You are a big stupid oaf.
You have a fan base of seven year olds and rednecks.
You are not as cool as you let yourself believe.
You are a wash.
Fuck you.
May your beer gut crush your lungs
And suffocate you in your sleep and "The Undertaker" Laughs.
You
You left the girl you loved
Because she

Was Hypocritical
Told you half-truths
about where she was going.
You are not who you say you are.
You are not in Love with me.
You are not Caring.
You are not capable of unconditional love.
You are not My Girlfriend.
You are not My Princess.
You are not My Baby.
You are not My Love.
You are a nineteen year old.
You are too busy having your fun.
You are too busy working out.
You are too busy karaokeing.
Forget it.
May your transformation into a Cockroach hillbilly
Be Kafkaesque in all ways.
You
You left the Girl you loved
But you
Can't seem to get over her
All thoughts, dreams
Are all about her.
You are not able to let her go.
You are not hating her.
You are not a strong male.
You are not Marlon Brando.
You are not James Cagney.
You are not Humphrey Bogart.
You are not Samuel Jackson.

- REALIZATIONS

You are a hopeless romantic.
You are always going to be miserable.
You will never find unconditional love.
You will never be wanted or desired.
Deal with it.
May your days be filled with drinks and song
And Lloyd Dobbler as a drinking buddy.

14

Monster Face

I hold a hundred thousand monsters at bay
   Each morning when I awaken
I keep them hidden behind a plaster mask
With a plaster smile on top
The monsters are cunning
Evil and quick
Plotting to overthrow
And as the hands tick past
They manage to find ways to escape
Through the cracks of the shoddy mask
Rearing their hideous faces
To play upon mine
And scare the ones I love.
When I was a younger man
I could pick myself out of a crowd
But now I am lost in a sea
Unsure of which face is my true face
And which is the face of the monsters
They make life difficult
They steal attempts at happiness
They despise me for being myself

MONSTER FACE

And never allow me
To shed the mask and show my true face.
In a way I am glad
My true face has been hidden in shadows
For a number of years
It has been beaten by the monsters
As it was shackled to the wall of my mind
It is probably a disfigured mess
Broken and beaten down
I am not sure if my true face could still show emotion
I am not sure if my true face could smile
But that is why the clown monster is here
I am not sure if my true face could be angry
But that is why the fury monster is here
The only thing my true face could show is sorrow
Grief and pity
Unhappinesss
But there is also a monster for that
That monster shows sorrow better than my true face
I know that my true face has vanished
And no longer exists
The monsters have killed it.
I am almost certain.
They have won.
But Have I become the monster
Or have the monsters become me?

15

On My Lips

A cigarette rests
    Next to the gun on my lips
Gotta finish the smoke
Before I blow my mind
After all
Cigarettes are expensive
You took the gun
From my mouth
Emptied the bullets
To the floor
Removed the cigarette
Snuffed it out
On the wall
Moved your lips to mine
And breathed new life
Into my soul
You moved your hand
Into mine
Led me from this
Dark and gloomy room
Led me to

ON MY LIPS

A bright song filled carnival
You showed me
What I'd never seen
You showed me
What I'd never known
You leaned in
Whispered in my ear
"You'll never be alone."
I couldn't help but
Fall in love with you
You made me happy
For a little while
The longest while
That happiness has given itself
To me
It had to end
The carnival had to
Dim it's lights
You had to
Flicker and fade away
I had to
Make my way back home
Pick up the snuffed out cigarette
Reload
Sit back down
Put the gun where it belongs
Resting
Next to the cigarette on my lips.

16

Real Rain Came

The rain falls in sheets
    Through this dense blanket of fog
The puddles grow larger
Fallen angels drown
You can not run
It will fall upon you
It is not racist
Not proud
Nor does it hold grudges
It will take you
It takes everyone
The walls are moving in
Making everything feel smaller
As the rain build up
Around my ankles
Moving higher
I try to run
But I can't
I try to escape
These tightening walls
All the doors are locked

REAL RAIN CAME

All the windows are shattered
Bars cover them
All buildings are burning
The rain is not helping
It weighs down the structure
They collapse
Raining plaster from above me
There is no escape
The water is higher
To my hips now
I stop trying to fight
I stand in silence
We all have to go sometime
On that trip
From the earth to the moon
I watch in terror
As my world ends
I can't even scream

17

Rambling

Bloodied Masses
    Horns and Tassles
Lost My Mind
Little Rascal
Don't Know Why
Sit and Cry
Barrel to my Head
Engulfed by Sighs
Pen is Bleating
No One's Reading
Here an Explosion
Soul Seceding
Eyes are Burning
Hands are Yearning
Lay in Bed
Toss and Turning
Dreams are Going
Time is Blowing
Hair a Mess
Wound is Showing
Life is less

Worst is Best
Days a Quiz
Made Wrong Guess
Tears are Red
Done is Said
Time Ticked By
Now I'm Dead
Things Same Old
Lost My Soul
Down in a Box
Dirt in a Hole.

18
Lost

Don't leave
    Without saying good-bye
Don't leave
Without saying you love me
I will try
To do the same for you
You're already gone
The world looms out before me
Covered in a thick fog
I have no clue
As to where I am going
I have no clue
As to where I have been
I have no clue
How I got to the point that I am at
I have floated
In and around this world
Like the wind
With nothing more
Than a handful of friends
Shoulders to cry on

- LOST

I am lacking
Shoulders to lean on
I have none
No one who loves me
No one who can save me
No one to rebuild
The havoc I am
The world will keep spinning
This world around me
Will spin until there is nothing left
I want to leave here
I want to go somewhere
I don't want to go home
No one cares in this world
So grows the hatred
I have nothing
Nothing to live for.

19

Life, From a Different Point of View

Standing atop a golden mountain
    Looking down at fellow man
No idea where we're stopping
No idea how to slow.
Little devils creep behind you
No idea that they're present
Push you quickly without thinking
And you plummet towards below.
Now you know where you'll be stopping,
On the jagged rocks below.
With no hope or chance to slow.
Fellow man is looking at you
Laughing out at your dismay
Laughing hard at your misfortune
They don't know what else to say,
Jagged rocks are rushing closer
You brace yourself against their teeth
Little devils wait and whisper
Hoping that their deed is done
Rocks tear into fleshy belly

Rocks tear into soft small eyes.
Rocks are spattered with crimson liquid
Rocks now know that man can't fly
Little devils see the blood spray
Little devils shout with glee
Little devils slip back to shadows
Little devils you can't see
Fellow man continue laughing
Fellow man who saw you perish
Fellow man refuse to care.

20

Idiotic

Day after day
    I stand in a hollow
Shell of a man who's a boy
Living my life
Like a fool
With no future
I feel so helpless
So worthless inside
I am slowly drowning
When I should be swimming
But not with the sharks
It terrifies me
To think that
I'll never
Travel upwards
Grab hold of a star
Way up there
So high
In the velvet
Black void
Above me

IDIOTIC

Taunting me
Laughing
Knowing I want it
Knowing I'll reach for it
Knowing odds are
When I do
I will fall.

21
Finis

He asked her out
She turned him down

She held a smile
He wore a frown

She stole his heart
And turned it black

She laughed at him
And gave it back

He lay down
   in misery

She ran off
Fuck chivalry

His body bled
His head still hurt

– FINIS

He soon would pass
Heart on his shirt

Sadness came
And stole his soul

He wept and cried
Hid like a mole

His life was gone
His love left, too

His tears fell faster
As he sat and cried

And drowned his sorrows
In cyanide.

22

Goodbye, Cruel World

The sun blew up at midnight
    On a world all silvery black
It tore apart both life and limb
Both never to come back.
The whole world was just sleeping
When the fiery rush there came.
It brought us all to ashes
The crazy and the sane.
Its awesome heat snuck up on us
Like a killer in the mist
We never saw it coming
As it smashed us with its fist.
Just hours before we moved around,
The happy and the sad,
We went inside and closed our eyes,
And then we woke up dead.
Fields of green reduced to soot,
Hills reduced to coal,
Sky of blue was changed to black
From the fire that burned and rolled,
Seas were dried up instantly

GOODBYE, CRUEL WORLD

When the fire swept 'cross the land,
All the living ceased to live
When caught by the searing hand.
No one saw the sun explode.
No one heard its cry.
No one warned the others.
Everything just died.
The sun blew up at midnight
On a world all silvery black
It tore apart both life and limb
Both never to come back.

23

Fascination

My World
Is being slowly
Engulfed
No Job
No Cash
No way of support
For the first time
Ever
I began to feel
Free
Independent
Like a human being
Like flesh
And blood
Now
The world
Is turning
On Me
I look off
To the west
At the red hue

Of the sun set
Like looking
At goblins
With eyes
On fire
I fear
My whole life
Horrible things await me
Around every corner
Bad tidings
Written in black clouds
Across the sky
Shadows lurk
To harm
My well being
I can not stop them
You can not stop mourning
What am I to do?
I want to be rich
I want to be famous
I want to be known
I want
I want to be something
Anything
I want
So much more
Than I'll ever take.

24

Black Hole

Run like the wind
   To the dark
To the hole
Cover your eyes
Close them tight
Close them now
Throw yourself in
Take the leap
Take the plunge
Let yourself go
Lose your pain
Lose your strife
Let the air pass you
Through your hair
Through your flesh
Feel the ground rush up
Coming at you
Coming to you
Feel it hit your body
Body bleeding
Body hurting

– BLACK HOLE

Lay silent in the darkness
Never moving
Never breathing

25

Dread

A feeling of dread
    Has washed o'er me
I don't know why
I can't comprehend
This feeling
Or lack thereof.
It cuts me
Deep
Like a shard
Of broken glass
Or twisted metal
Deep within
My gut
My heart
My skull
My breath is short
My body weak
My hands are shaking
Madly
I am seconds from convulsing
Madly

- DREAD

I want to yell
Madly
I want to weep
I want to return to normalcy
The way things were
When I wasn't walking
Like I was in a dream
That was a century ago
Maybe longer
I awake
Every morning
To gray
Clouds
Upon the sky
After a restless night
Without dreams
Perhaps there were dreams
I just don't remember them.
I've become lost
In the shuffle
Of the pathetic world
Around me
Has my life
Come to a close
Shouldn't the credits
Roll
I am unable to deal
With this feeling
Deep within me
I want to go home
And sleep

For days
And days
Life is
A shipwreck
In the middle of
A vast black ocean
All you can do
Is hold your breath
As your face is submerged.

26

"Apocalypse"

the sun shines high above us
    we cannot see the rays from above
blotted out by blood red clouds
raining fire from darkened skies
clouds are streaked with black
souls of the damned inhabit them all
souls that shriek out in unhappy torment
they rue the life given to them that was lost
demonic limbs erupt from lands unholy
they are burnt and broke apart
they work to pull up battered bodies
layered down with years of dust
the faces are forever damaged
stuck in awestruck works of terror
eyes are sunken, lips dissolved
clothes are ripped and torn and tattered
it is a drastic wasteland now
here on this summers evening in hell
bodies are feasting on other bodies
forming flesh wounds with their teeth
killing and dying dying and killing

solely to survive in death
no one gives a damn about them
no one gives a damn at all

27

A Chance Meeting in the Woods

A boy went walking through the wood
    And he came upon a treeless clear.
Empty, dark, and desolate,
The boy walked in with fear.
In the center of this wood less land
There stood a man engulfed in smoke.
It held a scythe in skeletal hand
And wore a ragged, dusty cloak
The boy was frozen solid
His fear had taken over.
The cloaked man moved his bony mouth,
"I fear your life be over."
The boy cried out, "This can not be,
I haven't lived enough.
I've never skipped, I've never danced,
Or done other happy stuff."
The figure shrugged his shoulders
And stood in deafening quiet.
The boy began to weep and cry
He simply could not buy it.

A Chance Meeting in the Woods

Death moved slowly towards him
Icy hands stretched out.
The boy could not turn to run,
He could not even shout
Death's hand caressed the boy's soft hair
And his eyes forever closed.
His soul was clutched in Death's strong grasp
And that's the way it goes.
His life had ended far to quickly
He hadn't done enough.
His life seemed like a failure
His life seemed really rough.
He'd lived just slow and steady
He thought he had forever
Death came along and proved him wrong
Another chance comes never.
He didn't rage against the light
He went away with calmness
He wished he'd left a dying trace
For his life to confess
So in a word for this poor boy
To those who didn't see him
Live your life full as you like
Live life in Carpe Diem.

28

Another Day

Sitting at my desk
    Bored beyond belief
Hoping we would get held up
By a homicidal thief.
Wishing that the people
Would spontaneously combust
Or an asteroid would hit the store
Or an out of control bus
I guess it would be fine
If a poltergeist appeared
Holding up it's human head
By it's human ear.
If a parasitic leech
Burst forth out of my skull
Spraying blood and brains about
On this boring walls
Then, perhaps, I'd be content
Or if a fly landed next to me
I think that I would watch the fly
As it were watching me
A staring contest with a bug

That I'm destined to lose
Perhaps I'll just stare at the clock
Or the hole in my shoe
I wish something would happen
But it never does
Still sitting at the desk I'm in
More bored than I ever was.

29

Pinocchio

I've been forced
    Through the Portal
Shoved
Through the Gate
I'm pretty sure
No way of knowing
For sure
Pushed around
Since I was born
Totally confused
Try to do it
My own way
I fail
Miserable
Forced to do it
Status quo
Like a robot
In a factory
I've stayed alive
By putting up
I was accidental

Straight from birth
Should've been
Erased
I wouldn't care
My life has been
Sorted
Back and forth
Like a game
Tug o' war
Yanked around
Left
Right
Back
Forth
To
Fro
Pinocchio had no string
To hold him down
I do
My strings are here
You can't see them
They weigh
Me down
A hundred pounds
A piece
They hold me down
Pull me to
My Grave
Each day I live
I die more
And more

Yet
I fight
Against these string
I pull
Against these shackles
I will
Wear them down
I will break them
I will
Win
Against these strings
Society
People
I will
Come out on top
I will
Come out as the victor.